DREAM CATCHER

THAT PALMISTRY HANBOOK

Insights from an Intuative Palm Reader
Interpreting Mysterious Dermaglyphs

Contents

One

THAT PALMISTRY HANDBOOK

Welcome and good fortune be with you!

Palm reading, also known as palmistry, has captivated the human imagination for thousands of years. From the bustling markets of ancient China to the opulent courts of Victorian Europe, palmistry has served as a bridge between the physical and metaphysical, offering insights into our deepest desires, fears, and potentials. This ancient practice, steeped in history and tradition, continues to intrigue and inspire those seeking to understand themselves and the world around them. My Name is Dream Catcher and I practiced Palm Reading as a busker on Pearl Street mall Colorado for a couple years around 2008-2010, some in Arizona before that and now reside in California. I am writing this handbook to offer some perspective for anyone interested in developing a skill with Palm reading. Knowledge is power and with power comes responsibility, so get ready to delve into the art of palmistry with a guide who has practiced the art for many years. My special insights will be in brackets so you will know my interjections from otherwise derivative information. I bring you… da da da daaaa…… THAT PALMISTRY HANDBOOK!

Two

A Brief History of Palm Reading

The roots of palmistry can be traced back to ancient civilizations. The earliest references to palm reading are found in Indian scriptures, where it was practiced as part of the broader tradition of Samudrik Shastra, the study of body features to predict the future. From India, the knowledge of palmistry spread to China, Egypt, and Greece.

In ancient China, palmistry was integrated with traditional Chinese medicine and philosophy. The Ming Dynasty saw a flourishing of palmistry as scholars and practitioners documented their findings and refined their techniques. In Greece, the philosopher Anaxagoras is credited with introducing palmistry to Western culture. The Greeks expanded upon the knowledge they inherited, with prominent figures like Aristotle discussing the significance of palm lines and shapes.

The art of palmistry continued to evolve during the Middle Ages and the Renaissance. In Europe, palmistry was studied alongside astrology and alchemy, forming a triad of esoteric sciences. The Victorian era witnessed a resurgence of interest in palmistry, with numerous books published and palm readers becoming fixtures in high society.

(The fate of every man is sealith upon their hand! This Biblical scripture suggests that our fate is inscribed in our palms. I personally perceive our dermaglyphs to be like a serial number for God. Like a snowflake not one the same but all alike! This is evidence of individuality and instrumental to accountability. I got interested in Palm reading because of my interest in us as a whole. This art is analytical and spiritual.)

Three

The Cultural Significance of Palmistry Across Different Civilizations

P almistry has held a place of importance in various cultures, each adding its unique interpretation and practices.

- **India:** In India, palmistry was closely linked to astrology and spirituality. It was believed that the lines on the palm were a reflection of the cosmic forces at play in one's life. Palm readers were revered as wise counselors who could provide guidance on personal and spiritual matters.

(I Dream Catcher would like to share here that the palm leaf scrolls have indicated a journey of teachings for a young nomadic scholar "Breath of Life, or Yewe ben Yewe, Joseph bar Joseph ect... we now call Jesus learned mantras from Indian guru's Though the word Palm here references the wide supple leaves of a palm tree upon which the mantras were written, I hope to demystify the stigma surrounding Palmistry as an evil work from the devil. These rumors stem from a real history of Romanian Gypsy culture that you who seek supernatural information may incur curses that only silver coins aka payment can protect you from! As the Psychic, fortune teller, Medium, Reader ect…. You are willing to take on the responsibility of these forces for a price. I would avoid this tactic at all cost! As a practitioner, I use this history to pay homage to authentic experience so long as it is clear that the business of palmistry is guidance and wisdom and entertainment! Treat it as a service business! People want to be entertained, mystified and focused on! Why do folks go to a haunted house? Watch sci-fi movies? Go to a magic show? Insite number 1 is- don't make claims you can't back up! Avoid lawsuits or defamation. This is an intuitive art and not unlike a hairdresser or as my girlfriend who does Henna art on people at festivals is a service type business, be personable, give the customer what they expect while reserving the right to stay mysterious and coveted information like you would keeping your own secrets safe.)

- **China:** Chinese palmistry emphasized the balance of elements and the flow of Qi (vital energy) in the body. It was used to diagnose health issues and to understand an individual's destiny and character.
- (This is where the frailty and vital assessments are established. The Chinese systems are more doctor-like. Acupuncture and martial arts come from Asian medical doctrines! The Elements of fire, air, earth, water, are palm shapes and features. Wood and steel are names from Chinese palmistry)
- **Egypt:** In ancient Egypt, palmistry was practiced by priests and was associated with the divine. The Egyptians believed that the gods inscribed their will on human palms, making palmistry a sacred practice.
- **Greece and Rome:** The Greeks and Romans saw palmistry as a

valuable tool for understanding human nature and potential. It was used by philosophers and physicians alike to gain insights into an individual's personality and future.

- **Europe:** During the Middle Ages and the Renaissance, palmistry was practiced by scholars and mystics. In the Victorian era, it became a popular parlor game, but serious practitioners continued to study and refine the art.

Four

Overview of What the Reader Will Learn

In this book, "THAT PALMISTRY HANDBOOK," you will embark on a journey through the fascinating world of palmistry. You will learn to read and interpret the various lines, mounts, and shapes of the palm, uncovering the secrets they hold about your health, personality, and future. Here's a glimpse of what lies ahead:

1. **The Basics of Palm Reading:** An introduction to the main lines of the palm—the Life Line, Heart Line, and Head Line. You will learn how to identify these lines and understand their significance.
2. **The Life Line:** A detailed examination of the Life Line, revealing what it can tell you about your health, vitality, and major life events.
3. **The Heart Line:** Insights into the Heart Line and its connection to your emotions, relationships, and love life.
4. **The Head Line:** Understanding the Head Line's reflection on intellect, thought patterns, and mental energy.
5. **The Minor Lines:** An exploration of the minor lines, such as the Fate Line, Sun Line, and Mercury Line, and how they provide ad-

ditional insights into your career, creativity, and communication.

6. **Mounts of the Palm:** The significance of the mounts—Mount of Venus, Mount of Jupiter, Mount of Saturn, Mount of Apollo, and Mount of Mercury—and what they reveal about personality traits and strengths.

7. **Finger Shapes and Meanings:** Analysis of finger shapes, lengths, and phalanges, and how they indicate talents and predispositions.

By the end of this book, you will have the knowledge and skills to perform your own palm readings, offering profound insights into yourself and others. Whether you are a beginner or an experienced practitioner, "Hands of Destiny" will deepen your understanding of this ancient art and enhance your ability to uncover the mysteries written in the palm of your hand.

Chapter 1: The Basics of Palm Reading

Palm reading, or palmistry, is an ancient practice that interprets the lines and features of the hands to reveal insights into a person's character, life, and future. While there are many lines, mounts, and shapes to explore, understanding the basics is the first step. This chapter introduces the three main lines: the Life Line, the Heart Line, and the Head Line, explains how to identify them, and discusses the significance of reading the left hand versus the right hand.

(I would offer counsel in Love, Livelihood and Longevity. Relationships compatibility, Career options, health and wellness. If you are not a doctor, stick to having them look into areas of health and medicine. Or prescribe breathing exercises and stretching rather than pretending to have credentials. For all of these areas, read all the lines and the person then draw attention to the appropriate mount and line as you offer the advice. Also connect with the person with eye contact and ask questions about what you are sensing. For example, "You do a lot of outdoor activity don't you?" They most likely agree and give up information about the activities they like to do outdoors. If they say "Not really", then use this as an opportunity to give advice! I would say " Well here in your plane of Mars I see you would be fulfilling an affinity for nature. You may want to consider a camping trip or a planned leisurely hike in the near future". Catch my drift?)

Introduction to the Main Lines: Life Line, Heart Line, Head Line
1. The Life Line:
The Life Line is perhaps the most well-known and often misunderstood line in palmistry. It curves around the base of the thumb, encircling the Mount of Venus. Contrary to popular belief, the Life Line does not indicate the length of one's life but rather the quality of life, vitality, and major life changes. A long, deep Life Line suggests a robust and energetic individual, while a shorter or fragmented line might indicate a person who faces more health challenges or lifestyle changes.

2. The Heart Line:
The Heart Line, also known as the Love Line, runs horizontally across the top of the palm, under the fingers. It reflects emotional stability, romantic perspectives, and relationships. A deep, clear Heart Line signifies a person who is emotionally fulfilled and capable of deep, meaningful relationships. Variations in the line, such as forks, breaks, or chains, can indicate different emotional experiences or attitudes toward love.

3. The Head Line:
The Head Line starts from the edge of the palm between the thumb and forefinger and usually runs horizontally across the middle of

the palm. This line represents intellect, thought processes, and decision-making abilities. A long, straight Head Line indicates a logical, methodical thinker, while a curved line suggests creativity and spontaneity. Breaks or forks in the Head Line can signify mental conflicts or significant changes in thinking.

How to Identify the Major Lines on the Palm

Identifying the major lines on the palm is the foundation of palmistry. Here are some steps to help you locate the Life Line, Heart Line, and Head Line:

1. Positioning the Hand:

Hold the hand you are reading at a comfortable angle, ensuring it is relaxed. It's important that the hand is not tense, as this can obscure the natural lines.

(I sometimes have you put your palms together and then open them like a book. The heartlines meet together making a cradle and I can see the whole picture. I then might place a power object in your hands like a fiber optic sphere in your hands as a magnifier. Prisms work well but this is optional stuff. Plenty of light is most essential so the smaller details can be seen.)

2. Locating the Life Line:

Look for the line that curves around the base of the thumb. It typically starts between the thumb and index finger and arcs towards the wrist. This is the Life Line.

3. Finding the Heart Line:

Identify the line running horizontally across the upper palm, beneath the fingers. This line may start under the little finger (pinky) and extend towards the index finger or middle finger. This is the Heart Line.

4. Spotting the Head Line:

Look for a line starting between the thumb and index finger, usually running horizontally or slightly diagonally across the middle of the palm. This is the Head Line. It may be connected to the Life Line at its starting point or separate from it.

The Significance of the Left Hand vs. the Right Hand

In palmistry, the left and right hands serve different purposes and offer unique insights. Understanding the significance of each hand can enhance your reading accuracy.

1. The Dominant Hand:

The dominant hand (the one a person writes with) is often referred to as the "active" or "present" hand. It reflects the individual's current state, actions, and the path they are actively taking in life. For most people, this is their right hand.

2. The Non-Dominant Hand:

The non-dominant hand is known as the "passive" or "past" hand. It represents inherent characteristics, potential, and the person's innate nature. This hand is believed to show what a person was born with and their unaltered potential.

3. Comparing Both Hands:

By comparing the lines on both hands, a palm reader can gain a deeper understanding of how a person's life path has evolved. Differences between the hands can highlight changes in character, growth, and the influence of life experiences. For example, if the Life Line on the dominant hand is more fragmented than on the non-dominant hand, it might indicate that the person has faced more challenges and changes in their recent life than what was initially destined.

Understanding these basics provides a strong foundation for further exploration into palmistry. By learning to identify the major lines and appreciating the significance of each hand, you can begin to uncover the intricate stories told by the hands, offering insights into a person's past, present, and potential future.

Chapter 2: The Life Line

The Life Line is one of the most significant lines in palmistry, offering profound insights into a person's health, vitality, and major life events. Contrary to popular belief, it does not predict the exact length of one's life but provides a detailed map of one's journey, highlighting physical and emotional resilience, significant changes, and potential health issues. This chapter delves into the intricacies of the Life Line, exploring what it reveals about an individual's life and the various interpretations of its different forms and patterns.

Detailed Examination of the Life Line

The Life Line typically starts between the thumb and index finger, curving around the base of the thumb and ending near the wrist. It encircles the Mount of Venus, an area of the palm associated with love, sensuality, and vitality.

1. Identifying the Life Line:

Look for a curved line that begins between the thumb and index finger.

The line usually arcs downward, forming a semicircle around the Mount of Venus.

The starting point and the depth of the curve can vary from person to person.

2. Analyzing the Length and Depth:

A long, deep Life Line suggests strong vitality and a robust constitution.

A short Life Line does not necessarily indicate a short life but may suggest a person who conserves their energy or leads a more cautious life.

The depth of the line reflects the individual's vigor and enthusiasm for life; deeper lines indicate greater physical strength and vitality.

3. Texture and Clarity:

A clear, well-defined Life Line indicates a straightforward approach to life and good health.

A faint or broken Life Line can suggest periods of low energy or health challenges.

What the Life Line Reveals About Health, Vitality, and Major Life Events

The Life Line is a powerful indicator of a person's physical health, resilience, and significant life changes. Here's what various aspects of the Life Line can reveal:

1. Health and Vitality:

A strong, uninterrupted Life Line signifies good health and stamina.

Breaks, chains, or irregularities in the line can indicate health issues or periods of physical stress.

Forks or branches that emerge from the Life Line can suggest times when the person's energy is directed towards different activities or interests.

2. Major Life Events:

The presence of marks, breaks, or changes in the direction of the Life Line can indicate significant life events, such as major relocations, career changes, or traumatic experiences.

Islands (small circular or oval formations) on the Life Line can represent periods of illness, emotional distress, or significant challenges.

3. Physical and Emotional Resilience:

The consistency of the Life Line's depth and clarity throughout its length can show how a person handles stress and maintains their energy levels.

A Life Line that remains strong despite minor breaks or irregularities indicates resilience and an ability to recover from setbacks.

Variations in the Life Line and Their Meanings

The Life Line can take many forms, each with its own specific meanings. Here are some common variations and their interpretations:

1. Broken Life Line:

Multiple breaks in the Life Line suggest periods of upheaval or significant changes. These breaks could indicate health problems, emotional crises, or major life transitions.

If the breaks are bridged by secondary lines, it suggests that the person has support systems or inner strength helping them navigate these challenges.

2. Forked Life Line:

A fork at the end of the Life Line, also known as a "fork of travel," indicates a person who will travel extensively or relocate during their lifetime.

A fork near the beginning of the line can signify a strong connection between family influences and personal choices.

3. Chained Life Line:

A Life Line with chain-like formations, resembling a series of small loops or links, can indicate a life filled with emotional ups and downs. This pattern suggests a sensitive nature and a life marked by significant personal struggles.

4. Double Life Line (Sister Line):

A second line running parallel to the Life Line, known as a sister line or guardian angel line, indicates strong support from loved ones or a protective influence. It suggests additional strength and resilience.

5. Faint Life Line:

A faint Life Line may suggest a person who is more introverted or reserved, possibly indicating lower physical energy levels. It can also suggest someone who leads a less active or more cautious life.

6. Crosses and Stars on the Life Line:

Crosses intersecting the Life Line can denote major turning points or crises in life.

Stars on the Life Line can indicate significant achievements or moments of brilliance but can also warn of potential dangers or accidents.

The Life Line offers a fascinating glimpse into a person's life journey, health, and major events. By understanding the detailed examination of the Life Line, what it reveals about health and vitality, and the meanings of its variations, one can gain deeper insights into their own life and the lives of others. This foundational knowledge of the Life Line sets the stage for exploring the other major lines and features of palmistry, each contributing to a comprehensive understanding of one's life and destiny.

Detailed index for quick reference to specific topics and terms

Chapter 3: The Heart Line

The Heart Line, also known as the Love Line, is a vital component of palmistry that offers profound insights into an individual's emotional world, relationships, and love life. It reflects one's capacity for love, emotional stability, and the way one interacts with others on an emotional level. This chapter explores the significance of the Heart Line, how to interpret its various attributes, and what it reveals about relationships and romantic tendencies.

Understanding the Heart Line and Its Connection to Emotions

The Heart Line runs horizontally across the upper part of the palm, beneath the fingers. It begins at the edge of the palm on the pinky side and extends towards the index or middle finger. This line is a key indicator of emotional health, romantic relationships, and how a person expresses and experiences love.

1. Emotional Stability:

A clear and well-defined Heart Line indicates emotional stability and a balanced approach to relationships.

A faint or broken Heart Line can suggest emotional turbulence, difficulty in expressing feelings, or a tendency towards emotional insecurity.

2. Expression of Love:

The Heart Line reveals how one expresses love and affection. A deeply etched line suggests a person who loves deeply and passionately.

Variations in the line's texture and clarity can indicate different emotional experiences and levels of openness in expressing love.

3. Relationship Dynamics:

The position and shape of the Heart Line can provide insights into the dynamics of one's relationships. For instance, a Heart Line that curves upward towards the fingers indicates a person who is optimistic and idealistic in love.

A straight Heart Line suggests a more practical and realistic approach to relationships.

How to Interpret the Length, Depth, and Curvature of the Heart Line

The characteristics of the Heart Line—its length, depth, and curvature—offer valuable information about an individual's emotional nature and relationship patterns.

1. Length of the Heart Line:

Long Heart Line: A Heart Line that extends across the palm towards the index finger indicates a person who is highly affectionate, empathetic, and capable of deep emotional connections.

Short Heart Line: A shorter Heart Line, ending below the middle finger, suggests a person who is more reserved in expressing emotions and may prioritize other aspects of life over romantic relationships.

2. Depth of the Heart Line:

Deep Heart Line: A deep, pronounced Heart Line signifies a person who feels emotions intensely and has a strong capacity for love and attachment.

Shallow Heart Line: A shallow or faint Heart Line can indicate someone who is emotionally detached or cautious about forming deep romantic connections.

3. Curvature of the Heart Line:

Curved Heart Line: A Heart Line that curves upward towards the fingers reflects a person who is warm, sociable, and optimistic about love. This curvature suggests a playful and spontaneous approach to relationships.

Straight Heart Line: A straight Heart Line indicates a practical and logical approach to love. This person values stability and may prioritize rationality over emotional expression in relationships.

Relationship Insights and Love Life Predictions

The Heart Line offers a wealth of information about one's love life, relationship tendencies, and emotional patterns. By examining the variations and markings on the Heart Line, one can gain deeper insights into romantic inclinations and potential challenges.

1. Forks and Branches:

Fork at the End: A fork at the end of the Heart Line indicates balance and harmony in love, suggesting a person who can effectively balance their romantic life with other aspects of life.

Branches Off the Heart Line: Branches that extend upward from the Heart Line suggest moments of joy and fulfillment in relationships. Downward branches, on the other hand, may indicate periods of disappointment or heartache.

2. Breaks and Gaps:

Breaks in the Heart Line: Breaks or gaps in the Heart Line can indicate significant emotional trauma or disruptions in one's love life. These breaks may correspond to periods of heartbreak or significant changes in romantic relationships.

Gaps with Connecting Lines: If the breaks are connected by smaller lines, it suggests resilience and the ability to recover from emotional setbacks.

3. Chains and Islands:

Chain-like Formations: A Heart Line with chain-like formations can indicate a person who experiences emotional ups and downs, with periods of happiness followed by times of emotional struggle.

Islands on the Heart Line: Islands (small circular formations) on the Heart Line often represent periods of emotional distress or challenges in relationships. The size and location of the islands can provide clues about the timing and intensity of these challenges.

4. Stars and Crosses:

Stars on the Heart Line: Stars are rare but powerful markings that indicate significant emotional events or turning points in one's love life. A star can represent a deep, transformative love or a major emotional awakening.

Crosses on the Heart Line: Crosses can signify conflicts or challenges in relationships. The presence of a cross can indicate a need to address underlying emotional issues to achieve harmony in love.

Understanding the Heart Line and its various attributes allows for a comprehensive analysis of an individual's emotional world and romantic tendencies. By interpreting the length, depth, and curvature of the Heart Line, as well as the presence of specific markings, one can gain valuable insights into their own and others' relationships and love life. The Heart Line serves as a window into the emotional heart, revealing the nuances of how love and emotions are experienced and expressed.

Chapter 5: The Minor Lines

While the major lines—the Life Line, Heart Line, and Head Line—provide fundamental insights into a person's life, the minor lines add depth and detail to palmistry readings. These lines include the Fate Line, Sun Line, Mercury Line, and others, each offering unique information about specific areas such as career, creativity, and communication.

This chapter explores the minor lines, their significance, and how they interact with the major lines to provide a comprehensive understanding of an individual's life and personality.

Introduction to Minor Lines: Fate Line, Sun Line, Mercury Line, and Others

Minor lines, though less prominent than the major lines, play a crucial role in palmistry. They often reflect specific aspects of a person's life and can vary greatly from one individual to another.

1. Fate Line:

Also known as the Line of Destiny, the Fate Line runs vertically up the center of the palm, starting from the base and extending towards the fingers.

This line is associated with career, life path, and personal achievements. It indicates how external influences and personal choices shape one's destiny.

2. Sun Line:

The Sun Line, or Line of Apollo, runs vertically from the base of the palm towards the ring finger.

This line reflects creativity, fame, success, and personal fulfillment. A strong Sun Line suggests a person who will achieve recognition and success in their chosen field.

3. Mercury Line:

Also known as the Health Line or Line of Intuition, the Mercury Line runs vertically from the base of the palm towards the little finger.

This line provides insights into health, communication skills, and intuitive abilities. It can indicate a person's capacity for effective communication and their overall well-being.

4. Other Minor Lines:

Marriage Lines: Short horizontal lines located on the edge of the palm below the little finger, indicating significant relationships and marital prospects.

Travel Lines: Horizontal lines on the Mount of Luna (located on the lower outer edge of the palm), reflecting travel, exploration, and changes in life.

Girdle of Venus: A curved line above the Heart Line, suggesting heightened emotional sensitivity and creativity.

How These Lines Provide Additional Insights into Career, Creativity, and Communication

The minor lines offer detailed insights into specific areas of a person's life, enhancing the overall palmistry reading by highlighting strengths, challenges, and potential outcomes.

1. Fate Line and Career:

A strong, clear Fate Line indicates a well-defined career path and a person who is driven and ambitious.

Breaks, forks, or changes in direction of the Fate Line can signify shifts in career, changes in life direction, or significant challenges in one's professional life.

The presence or absence of a Fate Line can suggest varying degrees of career stability and external influences on one's life path.

2. Sun Line and Creativity:

A prominent Sun Line suggests a person who is creative, artistic, and likely to achieve fame or recognition for their talents.

Multiple Sun Lines or a forked Sun Line can indicate diverse talents and the ability to succeed in various creative endeavors.

A faint or absent Sun Line may suggest untapped creative potential or a person who finds fulfillment in less public forms of achievement.

3. Mercury Line and Communication:

A clear Mercury Line reflects strong communication skills, intuition, and the ability to connect with others effectively.

Interruptions or breaks in the Mercury Line can indicate periods of poor health, communication challenges, or disruptions in one's intuitive abilities.

The length and clarity of the Mercury Line can provide insights into a person's overall health and their capacity for maintaining good relationships and effective communication.

Interpreting the Interactions Between Minor Lines and Major Lines

The interactions between minor lines and major lines can offer a deeper, more nuanced understanding of a person's life. By examining how these lines intersect, overlap, or influence each other, a palm reader can uncover complex patterns and detailed insights.

1. Fate Line and Major Lines:

When the Fate Line intersects with the Life Line, it can indicate a person whose career is deeply influenced by personal life events and choices.

An intersection with the Head Line suggests that intellectual pursuits and decision-making significantly impact one's career path.

If the Fate Line touches the Heart Line, it indicates that emotions and relationships play a crucial role in one's professional life.

2. Sun Line and Major Lines:

When the Sun Line intersects with the Heart Line, it suggests that emotional fulfillment is closely tied to creative success and personal recognition.

An intersection with the Head Line indicates that intellectual efforts and creative pursuits are aligned, suggesting a harmonious balance between logic and creativity.

If the Sun Line intersects with the Fate Line, it signifies that career achievements and creative talents are closely connected, often leading to public recognition.

3. Mercury Line and Major Lines:

When the Mercury Line intersects with the Life Line, it suggests that health and communication skills are interconnected, impacting one's overall vitality.

An intersection with the Head Line indicates that intuitive abilities and communication are influenced by intellectual pursuits and mental clarity.

If the Mercury Line intersects with the Heart Line, it signifies that emotional health and relationships affect one's communication style and intuitive insights.

By understanding the minor lines and their interactions with the major lines, a palm reader can provide a detailed, holistic view of a person's life. These insights help illuminate various aspects of one's personality, career, creativity, and communication skills, offering a comprehensive understanding of their strengths, challenges, and potential future paths. The minor lines add depth and specificity to palmistry readings, revealing the intricate interplay of different facets of a person's life.

Chapter 5: The Minor Lines

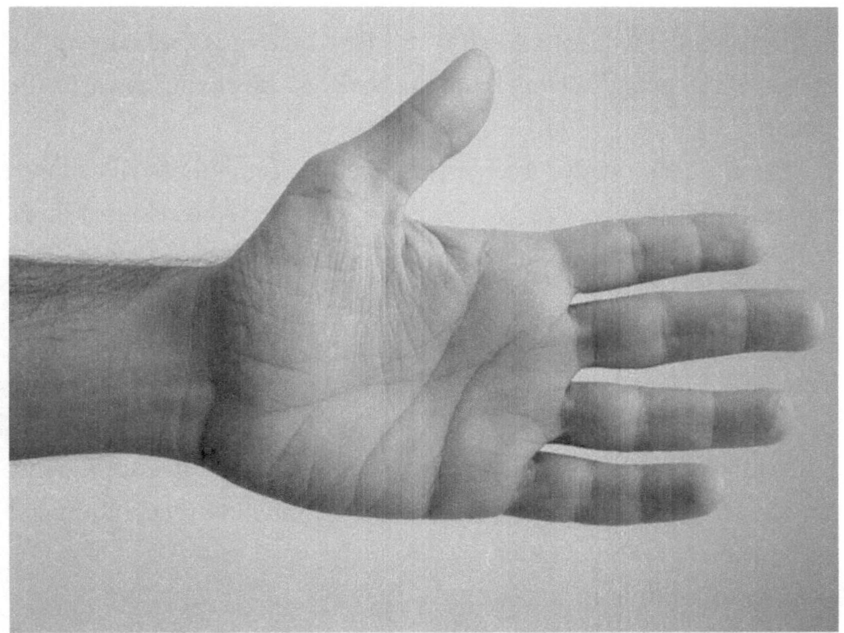

While the major lines—the Life Line, Heart Line, and Head Line— provide fundamental insights into a person's life, the minor lines add depth and detail to palmistry readings. These lines include the Fate Line, Sun Line, Mercury Line, and others, each offering unique information about specific areas such as career, creativity, and communication. This chapter explores the minor lines, their significance, and how they interact with the major lines to provide a comprehensive understanding of an individual's life and personality.

Introduction to Minor Lines: Fate Line, Sun Line, Mercury Line, and Others

Minor lines, though less prominent than the major lines, play a crucial role in palmistry. They often reflect specific aspects of a person's life and can vary greatly from one individual to another.

1. Fate Line:

Also known as the Line of Destiny, the Fate Line runs vertically up the center of the palm, starting from the base and extending towards the fingers.

This line is associated with career, life path, and personal achievements. It indicates how external influences and personal choices shape one's destiny.

2. Sun Line:

The Sun Line, or Line of Apollo, runs vertically from the base of the palm towards the ring finger.

This line reflects creativity, fame, success, and personal fulfillment. A strong Sun Line suggests a person who will achieve recognition and success in their chosen field.

3. Mercury Line:

Also known as the Health Line or Line of Intuition, the Mercury Line runs vertically from the base of the palm towards the little finger.

This line provides insights into health, communication skills, and intuitive abilities. It can indicate a person's capacity for effective communication and their overall well-being.

4. Other Minor Lines:

Marriage Lines: Short horizontal lines located on the edge of the palm below the little finger, indicating significant relationships and marital prospects.

Travel Lines: Horizontal lines on the Mount of Luna (located on the lower outer edge of the palm), reflecting travel, exploration, and changes in life.

Girdle of Venus: A curved line above the Heart Line, suggesting heightened emotional sensitivity and creativity.

How These Lines Provide Additional Insights into Career, Creativity, and Communication

The minor lines offer detailed insights into specific areas of a person's life, enhancing the overall palmistry reading by highlighting strengths, challenges, and potential outcomes.

1. Fate Line and Career:

A strong, clear Fate Line indicates a well-defined career path and a person who is driven and ambitious.

Breaks, forks, or changes in direction of the Fate Line can signify shifts in career, changes in life direction, or significant challenges in one's professional life.

The presence or absence of a Fate Line can suggest varying degrees of career stability and external influences on one's life path.

2. Sun Line and Creativity:

A prominent Sun Line suggests a person who is creative, artistic, and likely to achieve fame or recognition for their talents.

Multiple Sun Lines or a forked Sun Line can indicate diverse talents and the ability to succeed in various creative endeavors.

A faint or absent Sun Line may suggest untapped creative potential or a person who finds fulfillment in less public forms of achievement.

3. Mercury Line and Communication:

A clear Mercury Line reflects strong communication skills, intuition, and the ability to connect with others effectively.

Interruptions or breaks in the Mercury Line can indicate periods of poor health, communication challenges, or disruptions in one's intuitive abilities.

The length and clarity of the Mercury Line can provide insights into a person's overall health and their capacity for maintaining good relationships and effective communication.

Interpreting the Interactions Between Minor Lines and Major Lines

The interactions between minor lines and major lines can offer a deeper, more nuanced understanding of a person's life. By examining how these lines intersect, overlap, or influence each other, a palm reader can uncover complex patterns and detailed insights.

1. Fate Line and Major Lines:

When the Fate Line intersects with the Life Line, it can indicate a person whose career is deeply influenced by personal life events and choices.

An intersection with the Head Line suggests that intellectual pursuits and decision-making significantly impact one's career path.

If the Fate Line touches the Heart Line, it indicates that emotions and relationships play a crucial role in one's professional life.

2. Sun Line and Major Lines:

When the Sun Line intersects with the Heart Line, it suggests that emotional fulfillment is closely tied to creative success and personal recognition.

An intersection with the Head Line indicates that intellectual efforts and creative pursuits are aligned, suggesting a harmonious balance between logic and creativity.

If the Sun Line intersects with the Fate Line, it signifies that career achievements and creative talents are closely connected, often leading to public recognition.

3. Mercury Line and Major Lines:

When the Mercury Line intersects with the Life Line, it suggests that health and communication skills are interconnected, impacting one's overall vitality.

An intersection with the Head Line indicates that intuitive abilities and communication are influenced by intellectual pursuits and mental clarity.

If the Mercury Line intersects with the Heart Line, it signifies that emotional health and relationships affect one's communication style and intuitive insights.

By understanding the minor lines and their interactions with the major lines, a palm reader can provide a detailed, holistic view of a person's life. These insights help illuminate various aspects of one's personality, career, creativity, and communication skills, offering a comprehensive understanding of their strengths, challenges, and potential future paths. The minor lines add depth and specificity to palmistry readings, revealing the intricate interplay of different facets of a person's life.

Chapter 6: Mounts of the Palm

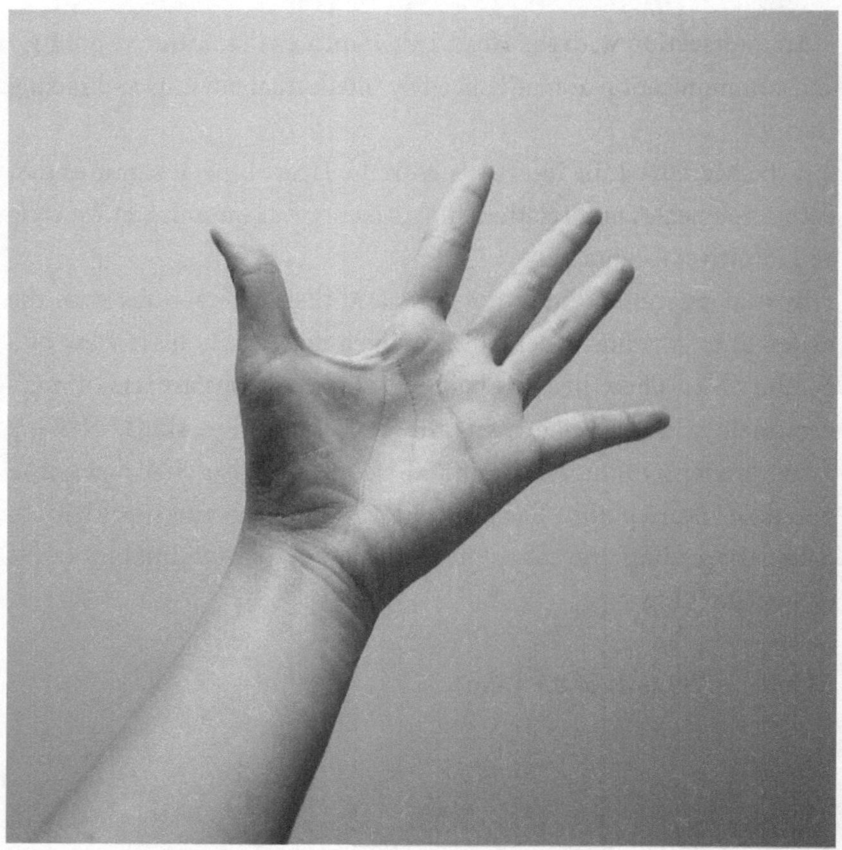

The mounts of the palm are elevated areas that play a significant role in palmistry. Each mount is associated with different planetary influences and represents specific personality traits and strengths. Understanding these mounts and their characteristics provides deeper insights into an individual's inherent qualities and potential. This chapter explores the significance of the primary mounts—Mount of Venus, Mount of Jupiter, Mount of Saturn, Mount of Apollo, and Mount of Mercury—how to identify and interpret them, and what they reveal about personality traits and strengths.

The Significance of the Mounts

The mounts are named after planets in astrology, reflecting their influence on different aspects of a person's life. Each mount is associated with unique qualities and strengths.

1. Mount of Venus:

Located at the base of the thumb, within the Life Line.
Represents love, passion, beauty, and sensuality.
A well-developed Mount of Venus indicates a person who is affectionate, sociable, and has a zest for life.
2. Mount of Jupiter:

Situated at the base of the index finger.
Represents ambition, leadership, confidence, and spirituality.
A prominent Mount of Jupiter suggests a person with strong leadership qualities, self-confidence, and a desire for achievement and recognition.
3. Mount of Saturn:

Found at the base of the middle finger.
Represents responsibility, discipline, wisdom, and introspection.
A well-developed Mount of Saturn indicates a person who is thoughtful, responsible, and values structure and discipline in their life.
4. Mount of Apollo:

Located at the base of the ring finger.
Represents creativity, fame, success, and appreciation of beauty.
A pronounced Mount of Apollo suggests a person who is artistic, creative, and likely to achieve success and recognition in their endeavors.
5. Mount of Mercury:

Situated at the base of the little finger.

Represents communication, intelligence, wit, and adaptability.

A well-developed Mount of Mercury indicates a person who is articulate, intelligent, and possesses strong communication skills.

How to Identify and Interpret the Mounts

Identifying the mounts involves observing their size, elevation, and firmness. Each mount's development can vary greatly among individuals, and these variations provide valuable insights into personality traits and strengths.

1. Identifying the Mounts:

Mount of Venus: Look at the area at the base of the thumb, inside the curve of the Life Line. A prominent, elevated area indicates a well-developed Mount of Venus.

Mount of Jupiter: Check the area at the base of the index finger. A noticeable elevation suggests a strong Mount of Jupiter.

Mount of Saturn: Observe the area at the base of the middle finger. A prominent, firm mount indicates a well-developed Mount of Saturn.

Mount of Apollo: Look at the area at the base of the ring finger. A raised, firm area signifies a strong Mount of Apollo.

Mount of Mercury: Check the area at the base of the little finger. A noticeable elevation indicates a well-developed Mount of Mercury.

2. Interpreting the Mounts:

Mount of Venus:

Well-developed: Indicates a passionate, sociable, and affectionate personality.

Underdeveloped: Suggests a more reserved or less affectionate nature.

Mount of Jupiter:

Well-developed: Reflects strong leadership abilities, ambition, and self-confidence.

Underdeveloped: May indicate a lack of ambition or confidence.

Mount of Saturn:

Well-developed: Suggests a thoughtful, disciplined, and responsible individual.

Underdeveloped: Can indicate a lack of structure or responsibility.

Mount of Apollo:

Well-developed: Indicates creativity, artistic talent, and potential for success and recognition.

Underdeveloped: May suggest untapped creative potential or a lack of appreciation for beauty and success.

Mount of Mercury:

Well-developed: Reflects strong communication skills, intelligence, and adaptability.

Underdeveloped: Can indicate difficulties in communication or a lack of wit and adaptability.

What the Mounts Reveal About Personality Traits and Strengths

The mounts provide a detailed map of an individual's inherent qualities and potential strengths. By examining the development of each mount, one can gain insights into various aspects of personality and capabilities.

1. Mount of Venus:

A well-developed Mount of Venus reveals a person who is loving, passionate, and enjoys social interactions. They have a strong appreciation for beauty and sensual pleasures.

2. Mount of Jupiter:

A prominent Mount of Jupiter suggests a person who is ambitious, confident, and has strong leadership qualities. They are often driven to achieve their goals and seek recognition for their efforts.

3. Mount of Saturn:

A well-developed Mount of Saturn indicates a person who is responsible, disciplined, and values wisdom and introspection. They are likely to be reliable and thoughtful in their actions.

4. Mount of Apollo:

A strong Mount of Apollo reveals a person who is creative, artistic, and likely to achieve success and recognition. They have a natural appreciation for beauty and are often drawn to artistic pursuits.

5. Mount of Mercury:

A well-developed Mount of Mercury indicates a person who is articulate, intelligent, and possesses strong communication skills. They are adaptable and quick-witted, often excelling in fields that require mental agility and effective communication.

Understanding the mounts of the palm allows for a deeper, more nuanced interpretation of an individual's personality traits and strengths. By identifying and interpreting these elevated areas, one can gain valuable insights into the inherent qualities that shape a person's life and potential. The mounts serve as a foundational aspect of palmistry, providing a comprehensive understanding of the unique characteristics and abilities that define each individual.

Five

Chapter 7: Finger Shapes and Meanings

Fingers are vital components in the practice of palmistry, each shape and length revealing unique aspects of a person's character, talents, and predispositions. By examining the fingers, we can gain insights into an individual's strengths, weaknesses, and elemental influences. This chapter delves into the analysis of finger shapes and lengths, the significance of different phalanges and their relation to elements, and how fingers can indicate various talents and predispositions.

Six

Analysis of Finger Shapes, Lengths, and Their Symbolism

Fingers come in various shapes and lengths, each carrying its own symbolic meaning. The general shape and length of a finger can offer clues about a person's nature and abilities.

1. Finger Shapes:

- **Square Fingers:** People with square fingers are practical, methodical, and detail-oriented. They value order and precision and are often reliable and trustworthy.

- **Pointed Fingers:** Individuals with pointed fingers tend to be intuitive, sensitive, and idealistic. They are often drawn to creative and spiritual pursuits.

- **Conical Fingers:** Those with conical fingers possess a blend of practicality and creativity. They are adaptable, resourceful, and have a balanced approach to life.

- **Spatulate Fingers:** People with spatulate fingers are energetic, innovative, and action-oriented. They thrive on excitement and are often involved in dynamic and hands-on activities.

2. Finger Lengths:

- **Long Fingers:** Indicate a person who is analytical, detail-oriented, and enjoys intellectual pursuits. They are often patient and thorough in their endeavors.
- **Short Fingers:** Suggest a person who is quick-thinking, intuitive, and prefers a direct approach. They are often spontaneous and action-oriented.

Seven

The Meaning of Different Phalanges and Their Relation to Elements (Earth, Water, Fire, Air)

Each finger is divided into three sections called phalanges, and each phalange is associated with one of the four elements: earth, water, fire, or air. Understanding these associations helps in interpreting the specific characteristics and talents indicated by the fingers.

1. Thumb:

- **First Phalange (Fire):** Represents willpower, determination, and leadership.
- **Second Phalange (Earth):** Indicates practicality, logic, and groundedness.

2. Index Finger (Jupiter Finger):

- **First Phalange (Fire):** Reflects ambition, confidence, and desire for power.
- **Second Phalange (Air):** Signifies intelligence, communication, and social skills.
- **Third Phalange (Earth):** Represents practicality, material success, and stability.

3. Middle Finger (Saturn Finger):

- **First Phalange (Fire):** Indicates discipline, responsibility, and focus.
- **Second Phalange (Air):** Reflects wisdom, introspection, and analytical thinking.
- **Third Phalange (Earth):** Represents structure, security, and material concerns.

4. Ring Finger (Apollo Finger):

- **First Phalange (Fire):** Signifies creativity, self-expression, and artistic talents.
- **Second Phalange (Air):** Indicates intuition, perception, and aesthetic appreciation.
- **Third Phalange (Earth):** Represents practicality, grounding of creative ideas, and material success.

5. Little Finger (Mercury Finger):

- **First Phalange (Fire):** Reflects communication, quick thinking, and adaptability.
- **Second Phalange (Air):** Signifies intellect, wit, and persuasive abilities.

- **Third Phalange (Earth):** Represents practicality in communication, business acumen, and grounding in ideas.

How Fingers Can Indicate Talents and Predispositions

The shape, length, and phalange structure of fingers provide valuable insights into an individual's talents, predispositions, and potential career paths.

1. Thumb:

- **Strong, Well-Developed Thumb:** Indicates a person with strong willpower, leadership abilities, and practical skills.
- **Flexible Thumb:** Suggests adaptability, creativity, and a relaxed approach to life.

2. Index Finger:

- **Long Index Finger:** Reflects strong leadership qualities, ambition, and confidence. These individuals often excel in positions of authority and influence.
- **Short Index Finger:** Indicates humility, a collaborative nature,

and a preference for working behind the scenes.

3. Middle Finger:

- **Long Middle Finger:** Suggests a disciplined, responsible, and focused individual who values structure and security. They often excel in fields requiring meticulous attention to detail.
- **Short Middle Finger:** Indicates a more relaxed attitude towards responsibility and discipline, often preferring creative and less structured environments.

4. Ring Finger:

- **Long Ring Finger:** Reflects creativity, artistic talent, and a strong desire for self-expression. These individuals often excel in the arts, entertainment, and creative industries.
- **Short Ring Finger:** Suggests a more practical approach to life, often valuing stability and security over creative expression.

5. Little Finger:

- **Long Little Finger:** Indicates strong communication skills, intelligence, and business acumen. These individuals often excel in fields such as writing, sales, and public speaking.
- **Short Little Finger:** Suggests a more introverted nature, often excelling in areas requiring focused, detailed work rather than public interaction.

By analyzing finger shapes, lengths, and the characteristics of different phalanges, palmistry provides a detailed understanding of an individual's inherent talents and predispositions. This knowledge can guide individuals in recognizing their strengths, overcoming challenges, and pursuing paths that align with their natural abilities and inclinations. Understanding the symbolism and significance of fingers enhances the overall practice of palmistry, offering deeper insights into the intricate tapestry of human personality and potential.

Nine

Chapter 8: Hand Shapes and Elemental Classifications

In the realm of palmistry, the shape of the hand is one of the first indicators of a person's inherent qualities and overall life approach. By classifying hand shapes into elemental types—Earth Hands, Water Hands, Fire Hands, and Air Hands—we can gain a deeper understanding of an individual's personality and how they navigate the world. This chapter explores the characteristics of each hand shape, what they reveal about personality traits, and practical applications of hand shape analysis.

Ten

Classifying Hand Shapes into Elemental Types

Each elemental hand shape is associated with specific physical characteristics and personality traits. These classifications are rooted in the traditional elements of Earth, Water, Fire, and Air, each symbolizing different aspects of human nature.

1. Earth Hands:

- **Physical Characteristics:** Square palms with short fingers. The palm is often solid and the skin is thick and coarse.
- **Elemental Traits:** Earth hands are practical, grounded, and reliable. They are down-to-earth individuals who value stability and security. Their approach to life is methodical and they tend to be hardworking and persistent.

2. Water Hands:

- **Physical Characteristics:** Long palms with long fingers. The palm is usually soft and the skin is smooth and supple.

- **Elemental Traits:** Water hands are sensitive, intuitive, and emotional. They are deeply in touch with their feelings and often possess a strong sense of empathy. These individuals are creative, compassionate, and highly adaptable.

3. Fire Hands:

- **Physical Characteristics:** Square or rectangular palms with short fingers. The palm is firm and the skin tends to be dry and warm.
- **Elemental Traits:** Fire hands are energetic, enthusiastic, and adventurous. They are passionate and driven, often taking the lead in various aspects of life. Their dynamic nature makes them natural leaders and motivators.

4. Air Hands:

- **Physical Characteristics:** Square or rectangular palms with long fingers. The palm is often bony with prominent knuckles and the skin is dry and rough.
- **Elemental Traits:** Air hands are intellectual, communicative, and analytical. They thrive on mental stimulation and enjoy engaging in conversations and debates. Their logical and rational approach to life makes them excellent problem solvers.

Eleven

What Each Hand Shape Indicates About Personality and Life Approach

Understanding the elemental classifications of hand shapes provides valuable insights into a person's personality and how they interact with the world.

1. Earth Hands:

- **Personality Traits:** Practical, reliable, methodical, and hardworking. These individuals are often drawn to careers that involve manual labor, agriculture, or any field that requires a grounded approach.
- **Life Approach:** Earth hands value stability and security. They prefer a structured and predictable life, focusing on building a solid foundation for themselves and their loved ones.

2. Water Hands:

- **Personality Traits:** Sensitive, intuitive, empathetic, and creative.

They are often found in artistic or healing professions where their emotional intelligence and compassion are valuable assets.

- **Life Approach:** Water hands approach life with a fluid and adaptable mindset. They are guided by their emotions and intuition, often seeking deeper connections and meaningful experiences.

3. Fire Hands:

- **Personality Traits:** Energetic, enthusiastic, adventurous, and passionate. These individuals excel in leadership roles, entrepreneurship, and any field that requires boldness and initiative.
- **Life Approach:** Fire hands approach life with a sense of adventure and excitement. They are driven by their passions and are not afraid to take risks to achieve their goals.

4. Air Hands:

- **Personality Traits:** Intellectual, communicative, analytical, and rational. They often pursue careers in academia, writing, technology, or any field that values intellectual prowess and communication skills.
- **Life Approach:** Air hands navigate life with a logical and rational perspective. They seek mental stimulation and enjoy exploring new ideas and concepts.

Twelve

Practical Applications of Hand Shape Analysis

Hand shape analysis can be practically applied in various aspects of life, from personal development to career counseling and relationship guidance. Here are some ways to utilize this knowledge:

1. Personal Development:

- Understanding your hand shape can provide insights into your inherent strengths and weaknesses. This self-awareness can guide you in making informed decisions about your career, relationships, and personal growth.
- For example, individuals with Earth hands can focus on building a stable and secure environment, while those with Fire hands can channel their energy into pursuing their passions and taking on leadership roles.

2. Career Counseling:

- Hand shape analysis can be a valuable tool in career counseling, helping individuals choose professions that align with their natural abilities and personality traits.
- For instance, someone with Air hands might excel in roles that require strong communication and analytical skills, such as a writer or a researcher, while a person with Water hands might find fulfillment in creative or healing professions.

3. Relationship Guidance:

- Understanding the hand shapes of yourself and your partner can enhance relationship dynamics by providing insights into each other's personalities and life approaches.
- For example, a person with Fire hands might need a partner who appreciates their adventurous spirit, while someone with Water hands might seek a partner who is empathetic and emotionally supportive.

4. Team Building:

- In a team setting, knowing the hand shapes of team members can help in assigning roles and responsibilities that match their strengths and preferences.
- For example, individuals with Earth hands might be well-suited for tasks that require meticulous attention to detail, while those with Fire hands can take on leadership roles and motivate the team.

By analyzing hand shapes and understanding their elemental classifications, you can gain a deeper appreciation of yourself and others. This knowledge can guide you in making informed decisions, improving relationships, and unlocking your full potential. The hands, as extensions of our being, reveal the intricate connections between our physical traits and our inner nature, offering a profound tool for personal insight and growth.

Thirteen

Chapter 11: Empowering the Palm Reader with Intuition

Palmistry is not merely a science; it is an art that blends intuition with empirical knowledge. As you delve deeper into the world of palm reading, you will find that combining your intuitive abilities with the technical knowledge from this book can significantly enhance your readings. This chapter will guide you on how to use the information you've learned to empower yourself as a palm reader, allowing you to confidently relate insights to your clients and create meaningful, accurate, and engaging readings.

Fourteen

Harnessing Intuition in Palmistry

While the lines, mounts, and shapes of the palm provide a solid foundation for interpreting an individual's personality, potential, and life path, it is your intuition that will bring your readings to life. Intuition, the ability to understand something instinctively without the need for conscious reasoning, plays a crucial role in palmistry.

1. Developing Your Intuitive Skills:

- **Meditation and Mindfulness:** Regular meditation and mindfulness practices can help you tune into your intuitive senses. These practices quiet the mind and open the channels to your inner wisdom.

- **Trusting Your Instincts:** During a reading, trust your initial impressions and feelings. Often, your first instinct is the most accurate.

- **Practicing Regularly:** The more you practice palmistry, the more attuned you will become to the subtle cues and energies of your clients. Practice with friends, family, and volunteer clients to sharpen your intuitive skills.

2. Integrating Intuition with Technical Knowledge:

- **Combining Observations with Feelings:** As you examine the lines and shapes on a palm, pay attention to any intuitive nudges or insights that arise. For example, while analyzing the Life Line, you might get a feeling about a significant health event that is not immediately apparent from the line itself.
- **Asking Guided Questions:** Use your intuition to guide your questions. If a particular aspect of a person's palm draws your attention, ask them about it. For instance, if the Heart Line suggests emotional sensitivity, you might ask, "Have you recently experienced a significant emotional event?"
- **Creating a Holistic Narrative:** Blend your technical analysis with your intuitive impressions to create a comprehensive and engaging narrative. This approach not only makes your readings more accurate but also more meaningful for your clients.

Fifteen

Insights for Different Age Groups

The age of your client can provide valuable context for your readings. Younger individuals often have palms that reflect potential and future options, while older individuals' palms can reveal tell-tale signs of their past experiences and professions.

1. Reading Young People's Palms:

- **Focus on Potential:** For young clients, emphasize the potential and possibilities indicated by their palm lines. Discuss their strengths, talents, and opportunities for growth.
- **Guiding Future Decisions:** Use your insights to guide them in making informed decisions about their education, career, and personal development. Highlighting their innate abilities can provide them with confidence and direction.

2. Reading Older People's Palms:

- **Identifying Past Experiences:** Older individuals' palms often show the impact of their life experiences. Look for signs of past professions, significant life events, and accumulated wisdom.

- **Guessing Professions:** Certain features on the palm can indicate past or current professions. For example, a well-developed Mount of Mercury might suggest a career in communication or business, while strong and square fingers could indicate a practical, hands-on profession such as engineering or craftsmanship.
- **Validating Your Intuition:** Use your observations to validate your intuitive insights. For instance, if you intuitively sense that an older client has had a challenging career, look for corresponding signs on the Life Line or Head Line to confirm your intuition.

Sixteen

Practical Applications of Intuitive Palmistry

Using intuition in palmistry can enhance your ability to entertain, guide, and interact with your clients. Here are some practical applications to consider:

1. Creating Engaging Readings:

- **Personal Stories:** Relate the palm lines to personal stories and experiences. For example, if the Heart Line indicates a deep capacity for love, share a story that illustrates this trait.
- **Interactive Sessions:** Encourage clients to ask questions and share their thoughts during the reading. This interaction can provide additional insights and make the session more engaging.

2. Providing Guidance and Support:

- **Empowering Clients:** Use your intuitive insights to empower your clients. Offer positive reinforcement and practical advice based on the palm's indications.

- **Emotional Support:** Many clients seek palm readings during times of uncertainty or emotional distress. Your intuitive empathy and understanding can provide comfort and clarity.

3. Demonstrating Your Abilities:

- **Accurate Predictions:** Use your intuition to make accurate predictions about your clients' past professions and experiences. This demonstration of your abilities can build trust and credibility.
- **Building Relationships:** Establish a rapport with your clients by showing genuine interest in their lives and concerns. A personalized and intuitive reading can create a lasting impression and encourage repeat visits.

Seventeen

Conclusion

Combining intuition with the technical knowledge of palmistry allows you to create deeply insightful and meaningful readings. By developing your intuitive skills and integrating them with the empirical aspects of palmistry, you can confidently relate insights to your clients, offering guidance, support, and entertainment. Whether you are reading the palms of young individuals with boundless potential or older clients with rich life experiences, your intuitive abilities will enhance your practice, making you a truly empowered and effective palm reader.

Eighteen

Chapter 10: Palm Reading in Practice

Palm reading, or palmistry, is both an art and a science that requires not only a deep understanding of the lines and shapes on the hand but also a strong ethical foundation and well-honed intuition. This chapter will cover ethical considerations and guidelines for professional palm readers, provide a step-by-step guide to conducting a palm reading session, and offer tips for developing intuition and improving accuracy.

Nineteen

Ethical Considerations and Guidelines for Professional Palm Readers

1. **Respect for Privacy:**

- Always respect the privacy of your clients. Keep the details of their readings confidential and do not share personal information without their consent.
- Be sensitive to the fact that palm readings can reveal intimate aspects of a person's life.

1. **Non-Judgmental Attitude:**

- Maintain a non-judgmental attitude during readings. Approach each client with an open mind and avoid making assumptions based on their appearance or background.
- Offer guidance and insights without imposing your own beliefs or values.

1. **Professional Boundaries:**

- Establish clear professional boundaries. Avoid forming personal relationships with clients that could compromise your objectivity.
- Do not offer medical, legal, or financial advice unless you are qualified to do so. Always refer clients to appropriate professionals for issues beyond the scope of palmistry.

1. **Informed Consent:**

- Ensure that your clients understand the nature of the reading and give their informed consent before you begin.
- Clearly explain what palmistry can and cannot do, and set realistic expectations for the reading.

1. **Ethical Pricing:**

- Set fair and transparent pricing for your services. Avoid exploiting vulnerable clients by charging exorbitant fees.
- Be honest about the length and scope of your sessions, and provide value for the price you charge.

Twenty

How to Conduct a Palm Reading Session

1. **Creating a Comfortable Environment:**

- Set up a quiet, private space where you and your client can focus without distractions. Ensure the area is clean and welcoming.
- Use soothing lighting and perhaps some background music to create a calming atmosphere.

1. **Introduction and Rapport Building:**

- Start the session with a warm introduction. Take a few minutes to get to know your client and make them feel comfortable.
- Explain the process of palm reading and address any questions or concerns they might have.

1. **Initial Observation:**

- Begin by observing the overall shape and texture of the hands. Note any distinctive features such as the shape of the fingers, the mounts, and the general appearance of the palm.
- Pay attention to the client's dominant hand (usually the hand they write with) as it reflects their current life and choices, while the non-dominant hand represents their potential and inherent traits.

1. **Reading the Major Lines:**

- Examine the three main lines: the Life Line, Heart Line, and Head Line. Discuss their lengths, depths, and any notable features such as breaks or forks.
- Relate each line to the client's life experiences, personality traits, and potential future developments.

1. **Exploring the Minor Lines and Mounts:**

- Move on to the minor lines (Fate Line, Sun Line, Mercury Line) and the mounts of the palm. Explain how these lines and mounts provide additional insights into specific areas of life such as career, creativity, and communication.
- Highlight any interesting intersections or interactions between the lines and mounts.

1. **Interpreting Finger Shapes and Lengths:**

- Analyze the shapes and lengths of the fingers and their phalanges. Discuss how these features relate to the client's talents, predispositions, and elemental traits (Earth, Water, Fire, Air).
- Offer insights into how these characteristics influence their behavior and choices.

1. **Combining Intuition and Knowledge:**

- Throughout the reading, allow your intuition to guide you. Share any intuitive impressions you receive, and use them to deepen the insights provided by the physical examination of the palm.
- Encourage your client to ask questions and engage in a dialogue. This interaction can enhance the accuracy and relevance of your reading.

1. **Summarizing and Closing:**

- Summarize the key points of the reading, highlighting the most significant insights and takeaways.
- Offer practical advice and positive guidance based on your findings. Encourage your client to reflect on the reading and consider how it might apply to their life.

1. **Follow-Up:**

- Provide an option for follow-up sessions if the client wishes to explore further. Offer additional resources such as books, websites, or workshops for those interested in learning more about palmistry.

Twenty-One

Tips for Developing Intuition and Improving Accuracy

1. **Regular Practice:**

- The more you practice, the more skilled you will become. Regularly read palms to refine your techniques and deepen your understanding.
- Practice on a variety of hands to gain experience with different palm types and features.

1. **Mindfulness and Meditation:**

- Engage in mindfulness and meditation practices to enhance your intuitive abilities. These practices help quiet the mind and allow intuitive insights to surface more easily.
- Spend a few minutes in meditation before each reading to center yourself and create a focused state of mind.

1. **Continuous Learning:**

- Stay informed about the latest developments in palmistry and related fields. Attend workshops, read books, and join professional organizations to keep your knowledge current.
- Learn from other practitioners and be open to new techniques and perspectives.

1. **Feedback and Reflection:**

- Seek feedback from your clients to understand how accurate and helpful your readings are. Reflect on this feedback to identify areas for improvement.
- Keep a journal of your readings, noting any intuitive impressions and their outcomes. This practice can help you track your progress and enhance your skills.

1. **Building Trust:**

- Trust in your abilities and the process of palmistry. Confidence in your skills will enhance your readings and help you connect more deeply with your clients.
- Remember that intuition is a natural ability that can be developed with practice and patience. Trust your instincts and let them guide you.

By combining ethical practices, a structured approach to palm reading, and the development of your intuition, you can provide meaningful and insightful readings to your clients. As you continue to hone your skills and expand your knowledge, you will become a more confident and effective palm reader, capable of offering guidance, entertainment, and deep personal insights to those who seek your services.

40

Twenty-Two

Chapter 11: Dream Child's Guide to Intuitive Arts

Palmistry is an ancient art that provides a profound window into the human soul, revealing our past, present, and potential future. As a palm reader, your ability to interpret the lines and shapes on a person's hand can offer deep insights into their character and life journey. However, the true power of palmistry lies in combining this knowledge with your intuition. In this chapter, we will explore how to use the information from this book to empower yourself as a palm reader, confidently relating insights to your clients by adding intuitive elements. We will also discuss how to interpret the palms of young people, revealing their future potential, and older individuals, uncovering their past experiences and professions.

Twenty-Three

Empowering the Palm Reader: Combining Knowledge and Intuition

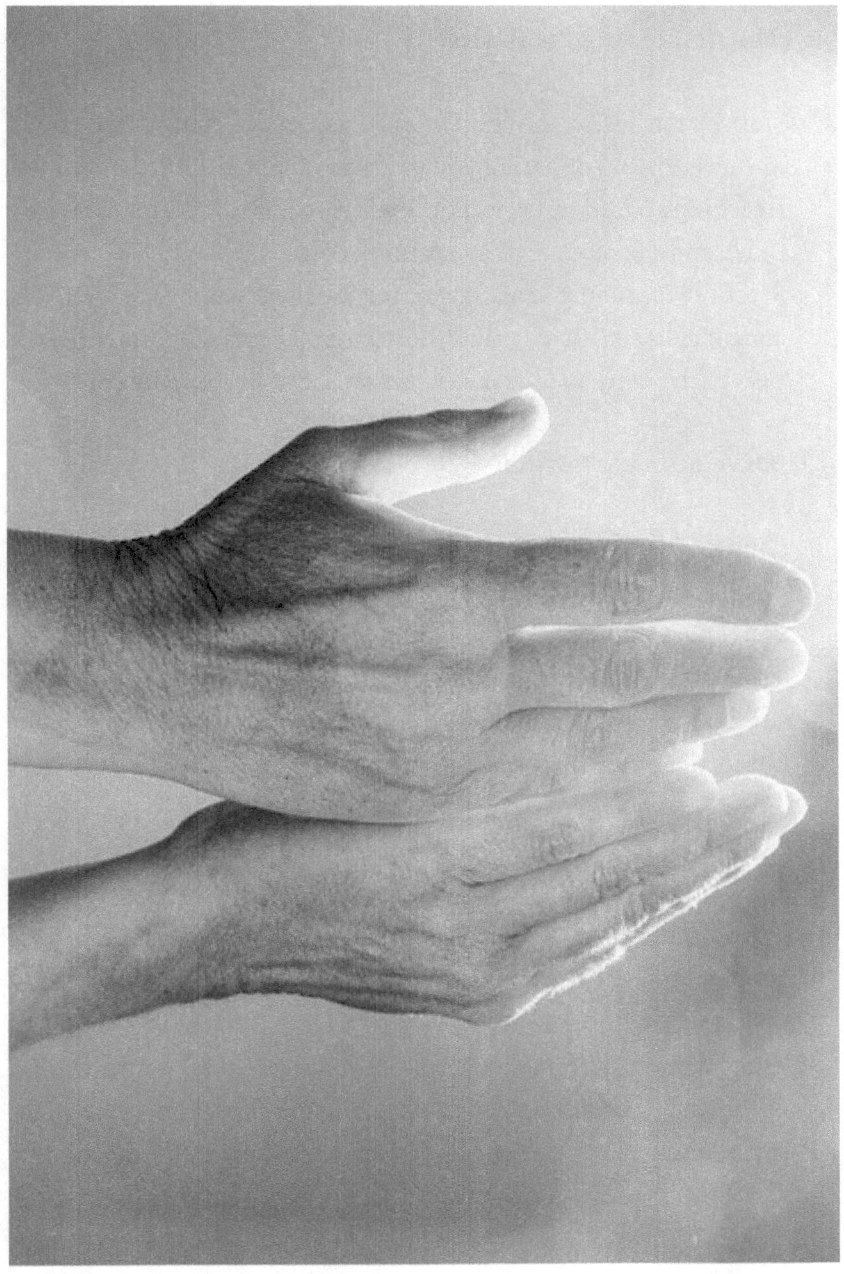

1. **Understanding the Basics:**

- Start by mastering the fundamental aspects of palmistry detailed in this book. Familiarize yourself with the main lines (Life Line, Heart Line, Head Line), minor lines (Fate Line, Sun Line, Mercury Line), and the mounts of the palm.
- Practice identifying and interpreting the shapes of the hand, fingers, and phalanges. Recognize the elemental classifications (Earth, Water, Fire, Air) and what they reveal about personality traits.

1. **Developing Intuition:**

- Cultivate your intuition by engaging in regular practices such as meditation, mindfulness, and journaling. These activities can help you tune into your inner voice and enhance your intuitive abilities.
- Trust your gut feelings during palm readings. When you sense something significant, don't hesitate to share it with your client. Often, these intuitive insights can be the most impactful.

1. **Combining Knowledge and Intuition:**

- Use the structured knowledge of palmistry as your foundation. This provides a reliable framework within which you can confidently operate.
- Allow your intuition to guide you beyond the literal interpretation of the lines. For example, while reading the Heart Line, you might sense underlying emotional patterns that are not immediately visible in the lines themselves.

1. **Building Confidence:**

- Confidence comes with practice and experience. Start by reading palms for friends and family, then gradually expand to paying clients.
- Remember that palmistry is both an art and a science. It's okay to make mistakes as you learn. Each reading is an opportunity to improve your skills and deepen your understanding.

Twenty-Four

Reading the Palms of Young People: Potential and Future Options

1. **Identifying Potential:**

• Young people's palms often reflect potential rather than established patterns. Pay attention to the development of the major lines and mounts, which can indicate areas of strength and future growth.

• Look for signs of creativity, leadership, and adaptability. Encourage young clients to explore their interests and passions, as these are often hinted at in their palms.

1. **Guiding Future Options:**

• Use your knowledge of palmistry to suggest potential career paths or personal development areas. For instance, a well-defined Mercury Line might indicate strong communication skills, suggesting a future in writing or public speaking.

- Emphasize the importance of flexibility and openness to new experiences. Young people have the advantage of time on their side, allowing them to experiment and find their true calling.

Twenty-Five

Reading the Palms of Older Individuals: Revealing Past Experiences

1. **Identifying Past Professions:**

- Older individuals' palms often show more defined lines and markings, reflecting their life experiences and career paths. Look for signs of wear and tear, calluses, and specific line patterns that indicate certain professions.
- For example, a heavily worn and callused palm might belong to someone who has worked in manual labor, while a smooth and delicate palm might indicate a career in the arts or office work.

1. **Interpreting Life Journeys:**

- Pay attention to the Life Line for signs of significant events, such as breaks, branches, or changes in direction. These can indicate major life changes, travels, or health issues.

- The Fate Line can reveal the stability and changes in their career path. A clear, straight Fate Line suggests a steady career, while a broken or wavy line indicates multiple changes or challenges.

Twenty-Six

Using Intuition to Enhance Accuracy

1. **Connecting with Clients:**

- Establish a strong connection with your clients by creating a welcoming and open environment. Listen actively to their questions and concerns, and use your intuition to guide the conversation.
- Personalize each reading by combining your intuitive insights with the knowledge of palmistry. This creates a more meaningful and impactful experience for your clients.

1. **Demonstrating Intuitive Abilities:**

- Use your intuitive skills to make educated guesses about your clients' past professions or significant life events. For example, noticing specific markings on the Mount of Mercury might lead you to suggest a background in business or communication.
- These intuitive insights can serve as a testament to your abilities,

impressing and engaging your clients. Even if your guesses are not entirely accurate, they demonstrate your commitment to understanding and connecting with them on a deeper level.

- (Dream Catcher hint) Intuitive ability goes beyond the reading of palms! What are they wearing? What is the person's hair cut like? I like to think of it like I am Sherlock Holmes and the tiniest detail can clue me into insights otherwise missed.

1. **Balancing Accuracy and Entertainment:**

- While accuracy is important, remember that palmistry also serves as a form of entertainment and personal exploration. Keep the reading light-hearted and engaging, ensuring your clients feel positive and uplifted by the experience.
- Use humor and storytelling to make the reading enjoyable. Share interesting historical or cultural anecdotes about palmistry to enrich the session.

Twenty-Seven

Practical Tips for Palm Readers

1. **Practice Regularly:**

• The more you practice, the better you will become at combining knowledge and intuition. Regular practice helps you develop a natural flow and rhythm in your readings.

1. **Seek Feedback:**

• Encourage your clients to provide feedback on your readings. Constructive feedback can help you refine your skills and build confidence.
• (Dream Catcher Hint) If they share a detail about their job or concerns about their love life then ask and share more into that subject. Allow the conversation to lead and the palm to confirm. This is an opportunity to suggest what salutations are represented in their hand! The secret is that the individual is the solution for

their obstacle. Their fate is in their own hands! Don't tell, show, don't take them to the destination, point the way.)

1. **Stay Open-Minded:**

- Every palm is unique, and every reading is a learning opportunity. Stay open-minded and curious, and continue to expand your knowledge and intuitive abilities.
- (D.C. Hint:) It is not about you knowing something they don't! It is about seeking and you will find. Thank them for stopping and being open to get to know each other, flattery is good here but not required. This is a social art,be curious with them.Let them know they are going to be well in spite of whatever obstacles or questionable situations they are facing.

By integrating the comprehensive knowledge of palmistry with your intuitive insights, you can offer profound and transformative readings to your clients. Whether you are reading the palms of young people, revealing their potential, or interpreting the life journeys of older individuals, your combined skills will empower you to guide, entertain, and connect with them on a meaningful level. Embrace the art of palmistry with confidence and intuition, and let your hands reveal the mysteries and wonders of the human experience.

STORIES FROM THE AUTHOR

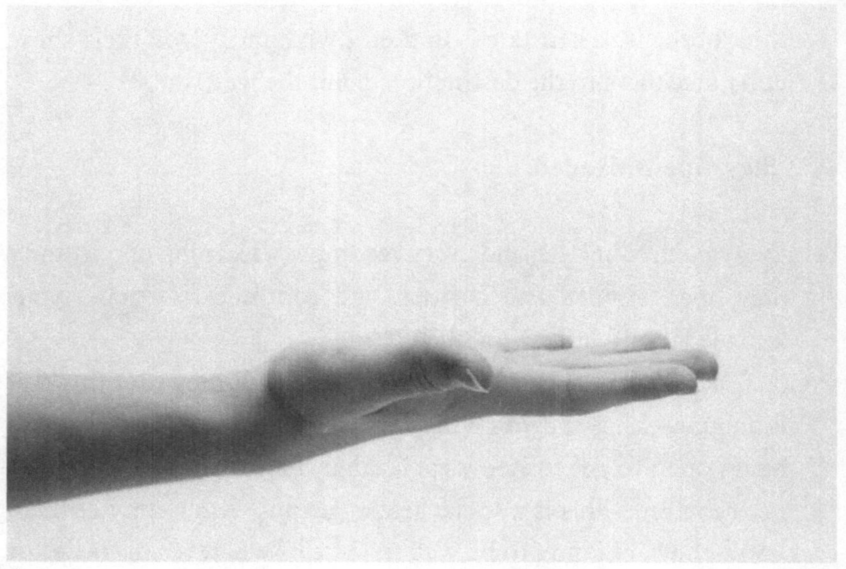

Fear Of The Unknown

One evening a group of four teen girls piled into the Wisdom wagon. They were giggly and having fun hanging out downtown on a Saturday afternoon. Welcome to the wisdom wagon. I am your palm reader Dream Catcher, I sense we all want a reading but someone here has a special question, yes?". The leader of the four began to explain that I was correct and they wanted their friend who was having a birthday to get a reading and that she was curious about her love life. I immediately could tell who was extroverted and that the birthday girl was the shy one. I offered the general reading for them at a group discount of $10 a head and so for $40 had the three girls who didn't have a birthday that day show me their palms. " I see you have been friends for some time already! And I see that you are the instigator aren't you? Was it your idea to come out tonight?'" already I am getting nods of affirmation from all the girls "And you over here krista, you are the sensible one helping keep everyone in less trouble? " She is looking puzzled and interested. "Because right here in your headline I read you are usually the most practical." I look to her friends to get confirmation. " Does Kristy remind you guys what time it is and sometimes turn down offers to go to a party where you don't know anyone?" They all get wide eyed and tell me instances where Kristy had more sense than the rest of them and helped them make smarter team decisions. " That's what I thought but look here on her life line! It has the indications of one who is very giving and nurturing to their friends." They all zero in on where I am pointing." But I also noticed right away that Cindy has water palms and academic skills like writing and arithmetic. Does she get better grades than the rest of you?" Now they are amazed! "Yes she does! She is valedictorian at our school!" says The leader Shannon. " Makes a lot of sense" I said thinking wow I am hitting the nail on the head! " Yeah her writers fork and the l

Minor dermaglyphs on her Saturn mount show that she could be in a place of recognition from her peers." I am gleaning the info they shared and building off of it a bit here now that I know she is valedictorian. "Lets see, what is your name again?" I ask the fourth young lady. "Tracy," she said. " "You are the birthday girl! Here let's do this,put your palms together and take three deep breaths with me" we do. " OK now open them like a book" she does. " Great! You have a deep well of emotion inside, I can see that you are very reserved but could really let loose if you are in a comfortable environment." She remains quiet but intense. "I see you are extremely loyal! I am sensing something about your family life." Shannon is giving me nods and signals that I am right. How is everything at home? Your headline and life line are greatly intertwined. I mean Your parents love you very much and I am guessing they will reward you well for being good." I didn't know at the time but I was touching on a too personal subject and was about to learn a lesson about keeping things in a certain direction. As the reading escalated Shannon was nodding and encouraging me with bits of info Tracy eventually starts to cry as Shannon, the leader of the quintet tips me an extra $20 and explains to me that I nailed everything to a T and that Tracy was already spooked about palmistry and the occult.

Also that Tracy had parents going through a divorce and it was an emotional time. Tracy eventually starts to cry as Shannon, the leader of the quintet tips me an extra $20 and explains to me that I nailed everything to a T and that Tracy was already spooked about palmistry and the occult. I really had never spooked someone to tears before but it was also a touchy subject I had uncovered by accident. Or was it? <twilight zone theme music>. I just hope that they had a fun evening and maybe decided to play Ouija board when they got home because being mystified and spooked can be fun too. That is unless Kristy the practical one votes against. ;).

A HAPPY MEDIUM

One evening a reporter for the Boulder city news rag shows up at the wagon. The paper is called THE DIRT. I will post a pic of the cover I was headlined on that week. He asked if he could interview me for the cover story or at least an article. I can't remember if I was aware it would feature on the cover. Anyway, I posed for the pictures with my fiber optic sphere and my Gothic eyeliner and finger less black knight gloves with candle and string lights. It was an awesome looking photo since the sphere warped my eye with its curvature. Here is what is strange. I had a brochure that made clear that what I do is Victorian style parlor game and guidance counsel style palmistry. For some reason the article was rewritten to make the interview a bit misrepresented. I guess it was a clever headline and for that I can forgive the article writer. The reason I felt misrepresented is because a medium is one who talks with the dead. A seance conductor if you will. I never claimed this. I honestly wanted to sue these guys for a moment but wouldn't know where I would start. Besides, I could lose and it never impacted me severely. I mean if I am saying that I offer advice from what your palm says about you and someone else says hey that guy is a witch and using black magic then it's just not true.I don't need religious fanatics boycotting me or judging me when I never made those claims is all. Totally Tabloid!. Like any art…don't let them besmirch you! All's well that ends well and I realized the intention was likely not vindictive.

Psychic Fair

I attended some fairs as a patron and got some readings of my own. I really liked some of the talismans and booths with art and such. I got a reading from a palm reader who taught me how to call abundance to me with a hand gesture. I won't divulge what the technique she showed me was because I consider it proprietary. However I thought it was cool to experience another palm readers' style. I thought I would be disappointed but I wasn't. I discovered she had books published and decades of experience so it makes sense that it was a decent reading. I would suggest the same for you. Try a few readers over the years. Palm, tarot, psychic. Get a feel for what was fun and how you can be a better reader. I made brochures, a sign and even a loop track with mystical indian music and a voice saying something like ask three questions and reveal your inner potential through the palm reader Dream Catcher. The recording didn't seem to make a difference but streaming some appropriate music can set the mood. Still remember, you don't have to make a business out of palmistry. You can share it with friends and family or for yourself!

SOCIAL BENEFITS LOVE LIFE LIVELIHOOD

Last story I would like to share with you is how palmistry enhanced my life. I had just returned to Boulder Colorado from a business trip and was invited to a birthday party that night in early November. It was a Scorpio event. A beautiful woman answered the door. "Hi I am Dream Catcher! My friends call me DC". I said I was not able to break eye contact. " Christine, nice to meet you". After a few moments of conversation about the birthday boy being a mutual friend and what a great turn out for the party I ventured in further to mingle and find a libation. As I found people I already knew and shared tales of my trip and how I had a chance to visit family in California and sleep under the twinkling stars a few times, I noticed Christine dancing near the band with serpentine motions. I had never seen such a mesmerizing dance before! I had to speak with her some more! Major, a man from the Caimen islands asked if he could give my business card to his friend who reads tarot and may have an opportunity for me . I gave him one.

I hung out with the birthday man Adam and we discovered that we both wanted to start a band! By the end of the night I had read a few palms because Major had opened up that conversation when he asked for my card. I flirted a bit with Christine and some of the other giggling ladies with tales of my trip and some free Palm readings. Before I knew it, Christine had disappeared and the party was coming to a close. I exchanged numbers with Adam and said my goodbyes.

A few days later I was in touch with the Lady who wanted to add a Palm reader to her street fair wagon and I started working there part time at 4 hr shifts. Then Adam and I began auditioning drummers and bass players for a reggae band! ADAMS' ATTIC and the Gone Jah Jug Band. And wouldn't you know it? Christine and I had even started dating and had a 5 year relationship before I relocated back to California! I hadn't realized it at the time but Palm reading had brought me the three things on every ones' mind all hinged upon one pivotal night! I got work, a lovely girl friend and the fulfilling joy of playing in a band. Talk about good fortune!

Conclusion

(Thank you for your time and interest. Now you have the information to read palms and an idea of what it entails. Be creative, use your better judgment and have fun. Make it your own and be honorable with your interactions. What I mean to say is keep palmistry in a good light. You will get better with practice but it really comes down to making it about the client, enjoying the social interaction, listening and serving them. Though there is an aspect of fortune telling it is Palmistry. Everyone you interact with is open to some sharing.. If you have crystals or other metaphysical skills, think of ways to display them in an integrative way. Clear your mind, do some mudra's between reading perhaps. And good fortune be with you!)

About the author;

Robert Paul LeBlanc, born in 1973, is known as Dream Child or Dream Catcher, a palm reader who has dedicated himself to studying palmistry styles dating back to the Ming Dynasty and Victorian era. Based on real life experience in Boulder, CO, USA, he practices his craft on Pearl Street at the Wisdom Wagonx3, a gypsy/wagon where tarot, palms, and auras are read by three practitioners, each bringing their unique expertise and heightened intuitive skills to their readings.

About the Author

Dream Catcher has lived in the US his entire 51 years of his life. Traveling to and through many states and living in the states of California, Colorado, Nevada and Arizona. Over the years he has become a skilled Palm reader, guitar player, pizza chef and writer.

You can connect with me on:

https://x.com/SkellingtonBuck